CHOOSE YOUR OWN ADVENTURE®

Fans Love Reading
Choose Your Own Adventure®!

"If you want to go on a magnificent adventure
of your choice, go to page 1 and begin reading.
If you don't then get another book!"
Quillyn Peterson, Age 9

"Come on in this book if you're crazy enough!
One wrong move and you're a goner!"
Ben Curley, Age 9

"I love the books because they are adventurous!
I love the surprise endings!"
Kaelyn Caprino, age 8

"Sometimes I'm scared because I
don't know what will happen. Then I just
make a different choice."
Natasha Burbank, Age 9

Illustrated by: Keith Newton
Book design: Jamie Proctor-Brassard of Letter10 Creative
For information regarding permission, write to:

CHOOSECO
P.O. Box 46
Waitsfield, Vermont 05673
www.cyoa.com

A DRAGONLARK BOOK

ISBN: 1-933390-56-5
EAN: 978-1-933390-56-7

Published simultaneously in the United States and Canada

Printed in Canada

0 9 8 7 6 5 4 3 2 1

CHOOSE YOUR OWN ADVENTURE®

SEARCH FOR THE DRAGON QUEEN

BY ANSON MONTGOMERY

ILLUSTRATED BY KEITH NEWTON

A DRAGONLARK BOOK

Your name is Wyrm and you are a young
dragon, called a Dragonlark. This might be the
biggest day of your whole life as a Dragonlark!

Turn to page 2.

You and your friends are on your way to the big hall in Smoke Mountain to see the treasures that just arrived. Two older dragons stop you on your way, with big news.
Bad news.

The Dragon Queen has been kidnapped! You and your Dragonlark friends are scared. Scared right down to your furry bones and the tips of your scaly tails. Two years ago three Very Bad Young Dragons vowed to take over the Queendom of Dragons, this wonderful, happy world you live in ruled by the Dragon Queen. They are the queen's young nephews. Nobody knows why they are so angry and mean or act so bad.

Now they have succeeded in carrying out their threat.

Your teacher Drakon meets with you. He is serious.

Go on to the next page.

"Lala, Windy, Gander, Wyrm, we need to go to the Great Hall right now. Instead of splitting up the treasures, the old dragons are going to make a plan to find the queen. Are you with me?"

You are smart, and brave, and are a natural leader. You pledge to find and free the Dragon Queen. But your friends look scared, especially Lala. She is the littlest.

"Lala, Windy, Gander! We can do it. We can save her." You are very excited. You almost forget about the fabulous treasure in gold, diamonds, rubies, silver, and armor on display in the Great Hall. What is all that, if the queen is gone?

Turn to page 4.

The Dragon Council meets in the
Great Hall surrounded by the treasure:
gold, jewels, a sailboat made out of silver,
pearls, diamonds, armor.

Turn to page 6.

The Very Bad Dragons who kidnapped the queen want the treasure, and they want to control all the dragons in Murfuss.

"Bring back our queen!" shouts the oldest of the Dragon Council. "We need her!"

Windy's cousin, Lacewing Swiftflyer, swoops down in front of the crowd of dragons. She is very special. She is known for her powers to find lost people, solve crimes, and make things right.

Go on to the next page.

"I declare everything postponed until our queen is found!" Earthpounder Thundertail, the head of the Council, roars over the murmur of the crowd.

You look at your friends, and you make your way toward the door with all the other dragons.

"Lacewing, where is she?" you ask.

"I don't know yet. It's a mystery to me," Lacewing replies. "I will cast a finding spell and begin the search."

"Wait!" Lala yells, grabbing your front leg. "I know where the Dragon Queen is! Or was two days ago. She was in the haunted part of the Ice Forest. If we hurry, she might still be there!"

If you look in the Ice Forest, turn to page 8.

If you choose to join Lacewing, turn to page 26.

"What were you doing in the haunted part of the Ice Forest, Lala?" you ask her as soon as you get out of the Great Hall.

"I was helping gather frozen fairy memories," Lala says.

"What are you waiting for?" Gander says gruffly, "We need to get searching!"

"He's right. Lead the way, Lala!" Windy agrees. "To the Ice Forest! Bring your mittens!"

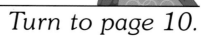

Turn to page 10.

"More climbing!" Lala groans, staring at the mountain you have to climb.

"Look!" says Windy. "A hot air balloon."

A hot air balloon is crumpled up on the mountainside. You climb into its little basket. The balloon has no air in it.

"It needs fire," says Windy. Everyone looks at you.

You breathe fire into the base of the balloon and the basket lifts off the ground with a WHOOSH and carries you up the mountain's steep face.

Turn to page 20.

"I didn't think it would be so cold," Gander says, blowing a small puff of smoke onto his paws.

"It is called the Ice Forest," Lala answers.

"Well, we've never been here," Windy says reasonably. "In fact, we aren't supposed to be here without a grown dragon, are we? How do we open the door?"

You look up and wonder the same thing. A giant door made of wood and ice towers above the four of you. Lala puts her shoulder against the door and pushes. The rest of you join her.

The door gives way with a clatter of breaking ice. A land of shining snow covering a rich spruce forest faces you.

You step through the gate.

Turn to page 13.

"What was the Dragon Queen doing here?" you ask Lala.

"She was talking to some fairies about reports of the Very Bad Dragons hiding in the Ice Forest."

"Fairies like those?" Gander says, pointing to a group of three fairies, sleeping in flowers. Their little shoes are tucked under and they look very peaceful, but there are icicles hanging off them.

"And look over there, dragon tracks! Big ones!" Lala shouts.

Turn to page 15.

"I think these little guys are under a spell," you say.

"Yeah, but what do we do about it?" Windy asks.

"We could try and wake them up," Lala says. "Fairies have special powers— *very special.*"

"Or they might get mad at us for waking them up. You never know with fairies. What about the tracks? We should follow them!" Windy argues.

If you try and wake the fairies, turn to page 29.

If you follow the dragon tracks, turn to page 42.

"We're ready!" You yell in your largest Dragonlark voice, which isn't very large.

The Very Bad Dragons laugh in anticipation of roasting you and your friends over their smelly, stinky dragon-fire breath.

"Now what?" Gander asks.

"What's that?" Lala asks, pointing at a dot in the sky. It grows larger quickly and you see that it is a dragon. And not just any dragon: **Lacewing Swiftflyer!!**

Turn page 19.

Lacewing Swiftflyer lands in a cloud of snow, and her expression is just as cold.

"I've had just about enough of you Very Bad Dragons–you Punky Roll, Billy-Butt, and you Barney Brainless. You three should be ashamed of yourselves. Hand over our queen and be gone! Don't ever come back!"

With that she throws dragon dust in their eyes and swirls her pointy tail. Next to Windy, the three Very Bad Dragons are small and helpless. Just bad teenagers again! They run off.

"We saved the queen! We saved the queen!" you all yell. You join the troll and his pet unicorn and head to the Treasure Ceremony, which will happen as planned. Thanks to you!

The End

Your balloon lands with a loud THUMP!

A giant eagle, <u>much</u> bigger than the giant in the castle courtyard, raises a wing, staring at you with a challenge in its eyes.

"So," Gander says, after dusting off the sand from Windy's abrupt landing, "when I was a baby, I would win all the Silent Contests by tickling everyone."

"Good idea, Gander!" Lala says, taking her tail and tickling it against the foot of the eagle.

You all scurry up a tree to reach the giant eagle. You tickle as hard as you can. Feet, claws, tail, teeth. Everything!

Finally, just as you are about to stop tickling, the eagle laughs. And it laughs so hard you all fly out of its nest and onto the hard rock of the mountain.

Turn to page 22.

"So, you got the eagle to laugh? First time for that!" says the Time-Keeper, a short elf who stands by a big hourglass. He hands a letter way up to the giant. The giant nods at the Time-Keeper, and then reaches down and flips the time glass over once.

"You can go back home," says the giant. "No one will ever know the Dragon Queen missed the Ceremony—because she didn't!"

"Catch you on the flip!" laughs the Time-Keeper, resting against his hourglass with a smile.

The End

"Well, no one was joking about the muck!" says Lala, shaking a splatter of muck off her toes.

You look around. Mud puddles burp and glump and fill the air with bad smells. Huge frogs croak and splash. There is a buzzing sound, like mosquitoes, in the distance. Something gluey and orange drips from a vine hanging in front of you.

Turn to page 70.

"VERY WELL, THE CUPCAKE IS THAT WAY," the giant murmurs, pointing at a sign that says Unsmashable Cupcake.

You see a great big cupcake with globs of frosting and rainbow sprinkles.

Gander gazes at the cupcake.
He loves cupcakes.

"O, Great Unsmashable Cupcake," you say, "show us the way to our queen?"

"Impossible. No queens allowed in our home. You will have to go back in time to find her. Good luck."

"Well, I guess we need to keep searching," you say. "There's always another day."

The End

"Lacewing, wait a minute!" Windy shouts.

"Come on," Windy says, grabbing your big claw and yanking you.

"Lacewing, it's me, Windy," Windy says, running up, "your cousin...."

"I know who you are," Lacewing says distractedly, "but I am on important DRAGON business, you wouldn't understand. Now run along with the other Dragonlarks and don't bother me."

Go on to the next page

Windy stops dead in her tracks and watches her cousin launch into the air and fly away in a blur.

"But Lala saw the queen two days ago!" Windy says, looking crushed.

"Right, and the queen mentioned getting something from the Sandcastle of Time and the Swamp of Endless Muck," Lala says into the silence.

"Why didn't you tell us that?" Windy asks, trying to hold back her anger.

"I forgot, but I remember now!" Lala says proudly.

"Fine, Windy-Arianis, your cousin doesn't want to help! We'll have to choose, the Swamp of Getting Stuck or the Sandbox of Time-Outs," you say.

Turn to page 28.

"DON'T CALL ME ARIANIS," Windy says through clenched fangs. "And they are called the Swamp of Endless Muck and the Sandcastle of Time."

"I don't like time-outs, but I do like muck!" Gander says.

If you want to go to the Ice Forest, where Lala first saw the Dragon Queen, turn to page 10.

If you choose to look for the Dragon Queen in the Swamp of Endless Muck, turn to page 23.

If you want to search in the Sandcastle of Time, turn to page 50.

"Wakey-wakey," Gander says in a baby voice to one of the sleeping fairies, shaking its shoulder with a rocking motion.

"What! Hiiiii-yah!" the fairy shouts, making a karate chop. You and your friends back up.

The other fairies wake up less angry, but still a little sour.

"Where's the coffee? I was told that the spell included a coffee," one of the fairies complains.

Go on to the next page.

"Did you bring cake? What? We're supposed to get cake," another adds.

"And puppy poo, but no one ever complains when that isn't here," muses another fairy.

"Okay, we're up, so what's it going to be? A wish or a finding spell?"

"What do you mean?" you ask.

"Whoever wakes us up gets one, or the other," yawns the fairy. "And then we go back to sleep!"

_____

If you ask for a finding spell to find the Dragon Queen, turn to page 62.

If you choose the wish spell from the fairies, turn to page 68.

You trust the troll. You don't know why, maybe it's just a gut feeling.

"Hey, you guys–er, I mean dragons, sneak over here," the troll says.

"This is my house," says the troll. "And my job is to guard the bridge! But the Very Bad Dragons overpowered me."

"So, what do we do?" you ask.

"The answers are in SqualPlendor."

"SqualPlendor!" says Gander. His teeth chatter. "I've never even heard of that place."

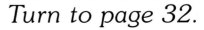

Turn to page 32.

"SqualPlendor is my homeland," says the troll. "I always find help there when I have a problem. Follow me!" It's steep and slippery.

"Don't let go!" Lala says as Gander lowers her down a cliff with his tail. "I wish I could fly!"

Sliding carefully, you inch over the edge and use your claws to grab onto the ice shelf below.

This is scary! You don't want to fall.

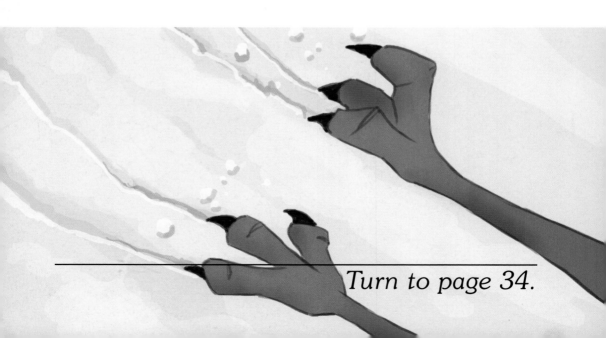

Turn to page 34.

"Jump, you chicken-dragon!" Windy shouts down from above.

"Fine," you mutter to yourself, letting go.

A small blast of flame escapes in a burp as you fall through the air, your little wings flapping as hard as they can.

"You did it!" Lala yells as you land. "The rest should be easy!"

The four of you cross the frozen river, and climb the gentler slope on the other side.

Turn to page 36.

You follow the road on the other side to the city of SqualPlendor, a place none of you have been to before.

The troll named Buttercup leads the way.

"You sure we should be going to SqualPlendor?" Gander asks timidly. He had a scary slip on the river ice.

"We've really got no other choice. We've got to save the queen!" you reply. The city guards, giant snow apes, let you in after checking your dragon credentials. Lucky you brought them.

Turn to page 38.

The city is a maze of twisted streets, falling-down buildings, and old trucks and cars. It's a mess. Giraffes, elephants and tigers wander the streets.

"We're lost," Lala says for the thirtieth time.

"Do we know if the queen even came this way?"

"No," you reply.

Turn to page 41.

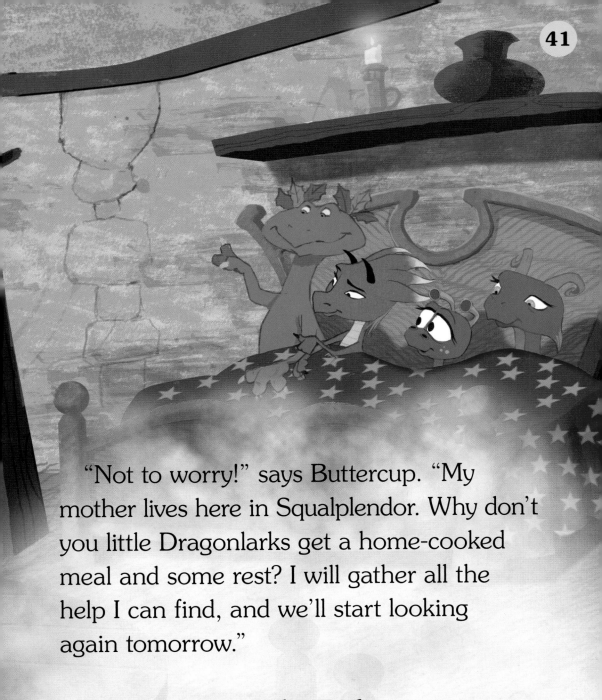

"Not to worry!" says Buttercup. "My mother lives here in Squalplendor. Why don't you little Dragonlarks get a home-cooked meal and some rest? I will gather all the help I can find, and we'll start looking again tomorrow."

The End

"Maybe we'll have time to come back and check on the fairies, but we need to stay focused. We are here to find the Dragon Queen," you say, bending down to look at the tracks more closely.

"I am hungry, though," Lala says, not paying attention to you. "Do you have snacks, Gander?"

"No. Sorry!" he says.

"I brought an ostrich egg my Nana packed for me!" Windy says proudly. "Wyrm, would you mind cooking it for us?"

"Sure," you say, blasting a small stream of fire at the giant egg. "All set!"

Turn to page 44.

The four of you crunch through the snowy forest, eating hard-boiled ostrich egg and following the dragon tracks that you hope will lead to the queen.

When you reach the frozen river, the tracks blend in with those heading to the stone bridge that spans the deep chasm.

"I've never been this far before," Lala says, looking at the setting sun, "and it's getting dark."

"Look at that little house under the bridge," Windy says, pointing to the stone house tucked under the bridge on your side. A thin plume of smoke comes out of a tidy little chimney.

Turn to page 46.

You get a creepy feeling that the Very Bad Dragons are not far off.

You hear your friends' teeth chatter with nerves. Shadows move around you. Could it be the Evil Ones?

Then comes a voice. "Two coppers each, please!"

You turn around and look up at a giant troll. He has a big nose. He sticks one hand out toward you, and in the other he holds a spiky club.

"Um, we don't have any money," Lala says.

"Then you can't pass," the troll says pleasantly.

Turn to page 48.

"Did the Dragon Queen pass this way?" you ask.

The troll shivers a bit. Maybe the Very Bad Dragons are watching. Maybe they have threatened the troll.

"Unfortunately, I have to respect my customers' privacy, so I can't tell you. Sorry. Can I put you down for four tickets at two coppers apiece?"

"We don't have any money," you say, again.

You and Lala look at each other with worry. Something is going on here.

Turn to page 59.

"Off to the Kitty-Litter Box of Time!"
Gander says, breaking into laughter.

Two hours later, no one is laughing.

"I'm, so, parched...can't go on much more," Lala says. There is no water in the Sandcastle of Time. No water at all!

"Can't be far now, that could be it, right ahead," you say, pointing to a dark shape on the horizon.

As you get closer the dark shape looks like a huge castle. Made of sand! It is the size of a mountain.

Turn to page 52.

After a long hike through the hot sand, you make it to the castle. A huge gate stands open to a courtyard.

In the middle of the courtyard sits a giant. He has hands the size of houses, and his head is like a rocky cliff. Smallish eyeglasses sit on the end of a long nose, and he makes notes on a notepad the size of a town square.

"WHO MADE THE APPOINTMENT WITH THE TIME-KEEPER?" the giant roars at you.

"Um, no one. We don't have an appointment," you say, shouting up to the giant. "We are looking for the Dragon Queen. Have you seen her?"

"SPEAK UP!" the giant replies.

Turn to page 54.

"Hey, let's ask that one! It's silly looking!" Lala says, pointing rudely with her tail at a giant pink frog with white speckles.

"I think you're 'silly' looking," sniffs the frog. "All those scales and claws, gets in the way, don't ya think?"

Windy interrupts their argument. "Do you know where the queen is?"

"Of course, I'll show you to Her Majesty right this way!" says the frog helpfully. "Wendy Mud-Gulper, at your service!" she says as she leaps away.

You all follow her.

"Not without Gander!" says Windy.

"I'm right here!" answers Gander, sticking his head above the muck. "Just enjoying this nice swampy muck."

Turn to page 56.

"WE ARE LOOKING FOR THE DRAGON QUEEN!" you yell as loudly as you can. "And could you stop shouting, please!"

"I'M WHISPERING!" the giant replies in another roar. "IF YOU DON'T HAVE AN APPOINTMENT, YOU'LL HAVE TO MAKE THE SILENT EAGLE ON THE MOUNTAIN LAUGH, OR SMASH THE UNSMASHABLE CUPCAKE!"

If you want to make the silent eagle laugh, then turn to page 9.

If you want to get an appointment with the Time-Keeper by smashing the unsmashable cupcake, turn to page 24.

"Just a bit farther!" Wendy Mud-Gulper tells you cheerfully after leaping from lily pad to lily pad in a giant pond. Carp the size of whales swim below the pads, making you a little nervous. They could eat any of you in one bite! Gulp.

"Here she is!" Wendy says proudly, bowing low before a giant yellow frog wearing a crown. Her arms are full of squiggling tadpoles. "Her Majesty Fly-Striker Pad-Leaper Supremo Ginormo the First!"

"Just call me Sammy," the queen says graciously, almost dropping a tadpole. "Whoops, Squirmer, quit squirming!"

"But we wanted the DRAGON Queen, not the FROG Queen!" whines Windy.

Turn to page 58.

"It's an honor to meet you though your Majesty," says Gander nervously.

"Oh, that DRAGON QUEEN. She's right there. Won't you say hello to my darling baby tadpoles?" The queen says, pushing the squirming tadpoles at you.
Lala screams.

Turn to page 60.

The words are barely out of your mouth when the troll suddenly turns into a ferocious fire-breathing, spark-spitting, stinky-breath dragon.

"HELP! SOMEONE HELP US!" you scream. "IT'S ONE OF THE VERY BAD DRAGONS!"

"More than one," comes an evil voice.

You spot two more fire-breathers coming out of the troll house.

A small troll creeps up to you and tugs at your wing. "I can help," he says in a small troll voice.

If you stand and fight now, turn to page 16.

If you go with the small troll, turn to page 31.

In front of you sits the Dragon Queen! Her golden scales glitter in the sunlight, her proud head stands tall in the wind, her beautiful white wings flap slowly, and she mouths the words "Help Me!" with her snout.

"There you are, my little Dragonlark darlings!" the Dragon Queen says to you in her fancy, silky voice. "My good friend Sammy, the gracious Frog Queen, has been showing me her children. All 22,654 tadpoles and 43,348 froglets. I've been here for days and days. What a treat!" she says, grinding her teeth together.

"Sammy, I think our time here has come to an end. I must lead these young larks back home!"

The End

"Find the Dragon Queen," you say, knowing that wish spells are all just a big scam. Who would give a wish spell for waking up some fairies?

The fairy in front of you puts her hand to her ear and then gets a far-off look as she pays attention. She stiffens and starts making weird noises.

"Bleep-Bloop-Bleep. Squaraglle. SSMM-MMEIIIRLLLL. Screech. <Pause>. Sorry. That party is not available right now. Please try another spell later. Code 5532. Thank you for trying FairAire. Always Aire, never Fair!"

"We don't have another spell," Gander says.

"Try collect?" Lala suggests.

"What's that?" you ask.

No spell. No queen. Return to GO.

The End

"I think this fort would make the perfect hideout for the Very Bad Dragons," you tell the group. "I bet they are inside."

"Let's hurry up, I'm c-c-c-ccold," Windy says as she tries to wrap her wings around herself.

A scream fills the air. Who could it be? Gander, or maybe the queen?

Turn to the next page.

"Gander?" you look around but it's too dark to see. Windy squeezes your claw.

"Over here, guys!" Lala shouts. "We found the orange frog! His name is Bartholomew Pond-Skimmer, of the MuckBowl Pond-Skimmers."

"Hi," Bartholomew says timidly, as a mud-covered Gander towers over him. "Joke's over, I see. Good fun, right? Dinner, anyone?" he offers, pointing to a plate of crickets and flies.

"What do you mean, joke?" you ask Bartholomew. "Do you know where the Dragon Queen is or not?"

You have a worried feeling in your gut as the frog looks around nervously with his bulging eyes. "Shhh," says Bartholomew. The Very Bad Dragons have stepped outside the fort.

Another scream penetrates the air. You see an amazing sight.

The queen has two of the Very Bad Dragons by the ear and is shaking her fingers at them.

"I told you to stop playing these games. If you don't grow up, I'll turn you into CATS! How would you like that? Now, let's go back home, all of us. Ally, ally in free!" she shouts.

With a purple flash you are all back in the big hall under Smoke Mountain. All is well in the queendom.

The End

"I wish I had a turkey/steak/chicken/ bacon/bacon/bacon/cheese/more bacon sandwich right now," Gander says soulfully, staring at his grumbling belly.

The karate chop fairy gives a big sigh. "In the old days, that would've counted. He would have a sandwich, and we would be done for the day...but, NOOOO..., now we have to play nice."

"Anyway, we wish to have the Dragon Queen come home," you say, wanting to cut Gander or another wish-making friend off.

"Done," says the fairy, sleepily.

"And I'll throw you in as conquering heroes for free!"

POP

You are back in the hall of the Treasure Ceremony, the Dragon Queen is there, looking confused, and you and your friends are being showered in confetti and thanks!

You have done it! You have found the Dragon Queen. You are a hero!

The End

"Come on in, guys! The mud is perfect," Gander says, waving you to come. Big clumps of mud are stuck all over him. "It's just the right balance between slimy and sticky!"

"Oh Earth dragons," Windy sighs. "So. If the Muck is endless, where do we start?"

Turn to page 73.

"Let's ask the frogs!" suggests Lala.

"I don't know anything about the Dragon Queen!" announces a giant frog on a lily pad in front of you. "Ribbit, ribbit, croak?"

"I think you do know something!" Lala shrieks.

"Gotta go!" shouts the frog, leaping away through the swamp.

"Follow that frog!" Gander yells, paddling through the mud after the fleeing frog.

The frog makes enormous jumps and Gander squiggles and squoggles on his stumpy dragon feet.

You chase after Gander and the frogs, but you lose sight of them. A fort looms ahead in the swamp. Did they chase Gander inside?

If you follow another frog, turn to page 53.

If you sneak into the fort, turn to page 65.

ABOUT THE ILLUSTRATOR

Illustrator Keith Newton began his art career in the theater as a set painter. Having talent and a strong desire to paint portraits, he moved to New York and studied fine art at the Art Students League. Keith has won numerous awards in art such as The Grumbacher Gold Medallion and Salmagundi Award for Pastel. He soon began illustrating and was hired by Walt Disney Feature Animation where he worked on such films as Pocahontas and Mulan as a background artist. Keith also designed color models for sculptures at Disney's Animal Kingdom and has animated commercials for Euro Disney. Today, Keith Newton freelances from his home and teaches entertainment illustration at the College for Creative Studies in Detroit. He is married and has two daughters.

ABOUT THE AUTHOR

After graduating from Williams College with a degree specialization in ancient history, **Anson Montgomery** spent ten years founding and working in technology-related companies, as well as working as a freelance journalist for financial and local publications. He is the author of four books in the original Choose Your Own Adventure series, *Everest Adventure, Snowboard Racer, Moon Quest* (reissued in 2008 by Chooseco), and *CyberHacker* as well as two volumes of *Choose Your Own Adventure® The Golden Path™*, part of a three volume series. Anson lives in Warren, VT with his wife, Rebecca, and his two daughters, Avery and Lila.